the journal for Emotional Eating

the journal for
Emotional Eating

A Guided Journey to Improve Your Relationship with Food

Mayuko Okai, MS, RD

**ROCKRIDGE
PRESS**

this journal belongs to:

Introduction

Dear Reader,

I imagine you holding this journal in your hands, full of hope, excitement, and maybe even some uncertainty or fear. Chances are you have been struggling with your relationship with food, especially when you're emotional or stressed, and you're looking for a mindful solution. You are likely to look to food as a source of comfort or as a distraction. But you also know that eating when you aren't hungry only offers temporary relief and, ultimately, may leave you feeling anxious, alone, or ashamed. Perhaps dieting on and off has exacerbated these feelings. By picking up this journal, however, you've already taken a step toward taking control of your health and ending the frustrating cycle of emotional eating.

I'm Mayuko Okai, a Registered Dietitian, yoga teacher, and founder of Food Liberation, an Intuitive Eating coaching program that helps mindful individuals heal their relationships with food and their bodies. Through my 12 years of experience as a dietitian, I have worked with thousands of patients and managed multiple teams in hospitals across Los Angeles. But even as I worked, I realized a key component in healthcare was missing: adequate emotional support. I believe that connecting with patients on an emotional level can have a life-changing impact.

Around the same time that I was assisting patients with nutritional solutions, I discovered that yoga was both grounding and uplifting for me. I knew I needed to dive deeper. When I became a yoga teacher, the doors to a new world of healing were opened. I soon shifted my nutrition practice to incorporate mindfulness techniques and began to focus on emotional care.

Since then, I have integrated Intuitive Eating with my experiences as a dietitian and yoga teacher to help individuals struggling with their relationship with food. Many of my clients experienced emotional eating on a regular basis before working with me. In my work with them, we dug down to the root-cause of emotional eating and found ways to manage the stresses that trigger eating as a coping mechanism. I'm delighted to say that the gentle management of emotions has been proven to heal again and again.

This self-guided journal includes prompts, exercises, affirmations, and mindful practices to increase self-awareness, rewire habits, and cultivate a healthier relationship with food. Work through the journal at your own pace. You can take it with you wherever you go and open it up whenever you have time to spare or when you need guidance. By using the journal regularly, you will learn to manage your emotions and break free from emotional eating.

Take a deep breath and let's begin the journey!

Reflect upon the times you have recently eaten in response to stress or to avoid your feelings. What emotions or situations triggered you? How often do you experience these emotions or come across these situations? How do you feel right after eating? How long does that feeling last?

_____

_____

_____

_____

_____

_____

_____

_____

_____

_____

_____

_____

_____

_____

_____

_____

_____

_____

Meet Your Inner Van Gogh

Choose a specific emotion that has led to emotional eating for you. Close your eyes and ask yourself what this emotion looks like. You can draw a picture of yourself or a representation of the emotion. Feel free to get creative, use colors, or include words. Don't overthink it. You don't need to be a great artist to express yourself.

Now, draw a picture of how you would like to feel every day. Compare the two drawings. You don't need to pretend that the first emotion doesn't exist. Remember, both drawings are expressions of you.

I am not my emotions; I only experience them. Tuning into my emotions gives me an opportunity to self-reflect and get to know myself better.

THE BOX BREATHING TECHNIQUE

The next time you find yourself turning to food for comfort, try this simple breathing technique. Know that it's okay if you end up eating afterwards. Breathing gives you an opportunity to pause and respond to your emotions instead of immediately reacting to them. It can be helpful to visualize the box below to guide your breath. Inhale through your nose for four seconds.

Hold your breath for four seconds. Exhale through your nose evenly for 4 seconds. Hold your breath for another 4 seconds. Repeat this 3 times. Notice how you feel afterward. Do you feel calmer? Are you more in tune with how you're feeling?

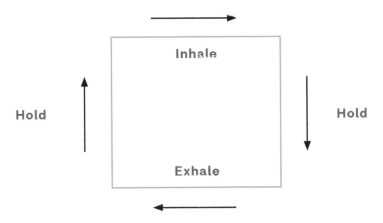

Fill in the blank: Feeling _____ is completely natural. I can learn to sit with any of my emotions and be okay with uncomfortable feelings.

Before you dive into managing emotional eating, it's important to become aware of your hunger. To start, reflect on the following questions: What am I hungry for right now? What have I been craving lately? Without judgment, write down the foods you would like to eat today.

The Hunger Scale

Hunger is an important survival mechanism that helps keep the body fueled and functioning properly. Ignoring your hunger repeatedly, whether intentionally to lose weight or unintentionally, can mask your body's hunger cues. This exercise will help you start listening to your body's hunger and honoring its need. On a scale of 0 to 10 (0 = not hungry; 10 = extremely hungry), how hungry are you in this moment?

I listen to my body's needs with compassion. I know I can restore my mind-body connection by practicing listening to my body patiently.

ONLY BITE OFF WHAT YOU CAN CHEW

Mindful eating helps you become aware of your relationship with food and your body. Consider putting these simple steps into practice the next time you sit down to eat.

1. Rate your hunger.

2. Remove any distractions. Turn off the television, put your phone away, and stay away from your email.

3. Take one bite at a time. Put your eating utensil down between each bite. If it's hard to remember to pause between each bite, try closing your eyes for a few seconds.

4. Savor each bite so you can notice the aroma, texture, and flavor of what you're eating. Notice any differences when you eat mindfully versus unmindfully, or without self-observation.

When I eat slowly and mindfully, I get to enjoy all the flavors of the food. Mindful eating helps me understand and deepen my relationship with my food.

Understanding your relationship with your body is a starting point in healing your relationship with it. It's important that you work on your mind-body connection to manage emotional eating. Describe your relationship with your body. What factors helped shape this relationship? What is your ideal relationship with your body?

_____

_____

_____

_____

_____

_____

_____

_____

_____

_____

_____

_____

_____

_____

_____

_____

_____

_____

_____

Love Your Body First

Pause to think about the different relationships you have with different parts of your body. Choose three to five parts of your body to reflect on. If there are body parts that are more uncomfortable for you to examine, choose those. What are the emotions or thoughts you associate with each body part?

Now, draw an image of your body below. On the image of the body, describe how you would like to feel about each of those body parts. This is an opportunity for you to practice self-compassion and gratitude in order to strengthen your mind-body connection.

I'm grateful for my body, for its strength and all that it can do for me. I'm grateful that my body helps me _____.

BODY ACCEPTANCE MEDITATION

This meditation helps you communicate with your body so that you can learn to accept and love it as it deserves. You can do this lying down or in the shower if you like.

Close your eyes, get quiet both inwardly and outwardly, and place your hands on one of the body parts you listed. Notice your reactions. Then, ask yourself what that body part does for you and express your gratitude toward it. Tell your body part that you love it, accept it, and will take care of it. Repeat this meditation with each body part you listed.

I know how to accept, appreciate, and love my body unconditionally. My body doesn't have to be a certain way for it to be loveable.

Having self-awareness means being in tune with your thoughts and emotions. As you tune in to yourself, you may find the same thoughts repeating in your mind. Ask yourself: What are the emotions I often experience? What are the negative thoughts on loop in my mind? Are there thoughts or emotions that I've been avoiding?

_____

_____

_____

_____

_____

_____

_____

_____

_____

_____

_____

_____

_____

_____

_____

_____

_____

_____

Learning Your Emotional Palette

One way to identify your emotions is to connect them to colors. Instead of trying to find words to describe your feelings, associating your emotions with different colors can make them easier to pinpoint. This can help you become more self-aware and less critical. Write down the emotions you experience often and the colors you associate with each of them. If using colors doesn't appeal to you, use other creative labels that are easy for you to remember.

EMOTIONS   COLORS OR LABELS

_____   _____

_____   _____

_____   _____

_____   _____

_____   _____

_____   _____

_____   _____

_____   _____

_____   _____

_____   _____

I welcome all emotions I experience. Having uncomfortable emotions does not mean I'm broken or unworthy. It is what makes me human. I am whole.

GET GROUNDED

Whenever you feel anxious, take yourself through this five-minute grounding meditation.

In a seated position, place your feet on the floor. Close your eyes and relax your entire body. Then, imagine roots growing from the bottom of your feet deep down into the earth.

Notice any sounds around you and let them be part of your environment. Then, connect to your breath. With each exhale, imagine that you are releasing what doesn't serve you into the earth beneath you. With each inhale, imagine you are bringing in what you need up through your feet.

I am safe. I am grounded. I am strong. I am centered. I am supported by the earth and sun. I have everything I need.

Our relationship with food during childhood can remain with us through adulthood. Reflecting upon your younger days, what emotions are most memorable? How did you express your emotions and your need for comfort? How did you cope with difficult emotions? Was food a major source of comfort then? Have you carried any of those habits into adulthood?

_____

_____

_____

_____

_____

_____

_____

_____

_____

_____

_____

_____

_____

_____

_____

_____

_____

Comfort Food

There's no need to worry if you associate your emotions with food. Eating is a coping mechanism that starts from the moment we are born. Babies cry and they're fed. This cycle of receiving comfort through food often continues in some way through childhood and into adulthood.

For this exercise, list your childhood comfort foods and write out any memories associated with each of them. Then, write down any emotions attached to each food or memory. If you have a small list, continue beyond childhood. If you recognize your current relationship with food in any of the listed items, draw a star next to it.

COMFORT FOOD   **MEMORIES AND EMOTIONS**

_____   _____

_____   _____

_____   _____

_____   _____

_____   _____

_____   _____

_____   _____

It's okay if emotional eating happens because that's what I learned growing up. I don't need to give myself a hard time about it.

MINDFUL COMFORT FOOD

For your next meal, choose something that sounds comforting or nourishing. Maybe it's a childhood favorite or a food that you associate with certain memories. Drop any judgment that's crossing your mind. As you eat this food, practice mindful eating (page 6).

Observe your thoughts and reactions. Does your chosen food taste the same as you remember? Does it evoke any particular memories? If the food tastes differently or doesn't bring up the same emotions as it did when you were a child, that's okay.

Just because I eat for comfort now doesn't mean I always will. I know that I'll find ways to manage my emotions more sustainably.

Let's examine your current relationship with food. The more awareness you have about your patterns and tendencies, the easier it will be to manage emotional eating. What is your current relationship with food? How do you feel about it? What is your ideal relationship with food? How would having that relationship make you feel?

_____

_____

_____

_____

_____

_____

_____

_____

_____

_____

_____

_____

_____

_____

_____

_____

_____

_____

_____

The Mindful Eating Pre- and Post-Meal Check-In

As you consider your relationship with food, take a moment before and after your meal to check in with your feelings and foster your mind-body connection. Ask yourself the following questions gently and with compassion.

PRE-MEAL CHECK-IN:

- [ ] How hungry am I right now?
- [ ] What am I hungry for?
- [ ] What judgments or criticisms do I currently have, if any?
- [ ] What is my intention for mindful eating?
- [ ] _____
- [ ] _____

POST-MEAL CHECK-IN:

- [ ] Did I enjoy my meal?
- [ ] How full do I feel?
- [ ] How satisfied do I feel?
- [ ] Did I connect with my intention for mindful eating?
- [ ] _____
- [ ] _____

I am in tune with my body and its signals so that I know when to nourish myself and what to nourish myself with.

THE MINDFUL EATING EXPERIMENT

This experiment is not your everyday mindful eating, but you can practice it occasionally to become aware of your relationship with particular foods.

▶ Pick one small food item you enjoy, like a piece of chocolate or fruit.

▶ If the food has a wrapper or peel, keep it wrapped or unpeeled. Place it in your hand and observe it. What are your thoughts? What is your body's response?

▶ Unwrap or peel as necessary and place it in your hand. What are your thoughts? What is your body's response?

▶ Take one small bite and set the food down. Observe the aroma, texture, and flavor. Chew slowly. What are your thoughts? What is your body's response?

Nourishing my body doesn't only mean eating healthy foods. It also means eating mindfully and being aware of my body's needs and responses.

Emotions can tell you a lot about yourself. Rather than ignoring them, it is helpful to acknowledge them and create healthy boundaries with them. Take an inventory of your recent thoughts and feelings. What are some emotions that you have been experiencing lately? Have you been avoiding or distracting yourself from any particular feelings?

Body Mapping

Ever notice how your head gets hot and your pulse quickens when someone's words or actions rub you the wrong way? Do you remember how it felt to have butterflies in your stomach when you passed your crush in the hallway at school? You may feel emotions in different parts of your body. Being able to identify the physical sensations associated with your emotions can help you be more in sync with your body. Where do you feel your emotions? How do they feel? For this exercise, draw one body shape above each emotion label. Then, draw on each body to express where and how you physically experience each emotion. Feel free to use colors, shapes, or words.

EXCITEMENT   CONFIDENCE

FREEDOM

SADNESS

BOREDOM

FRUSTRATION

I can learn from my body, which carries a wealth of wisdom. It knows when I'm feeling happy and when I'm feeling low.

MEDITATION ON MANAGING YOUR FOOD STRESS

Find a quiet place and get into a comfortable position. Close your eyes and take a few breaths. Visualize an emotion that usually triggers eating. Place your hands in front of you and imagine gently pushing it away from you. Observe the emotion again from afar. Is it familiar? How often do you have this emotion? How does it affect you? There's no need to avoid it or fight it away. Simply observe it from a distance. When you're ready, release the emotion and let it float away into the sky. Take three clearing breaths.

When triggering emotions visit, I don't need to give them the cold shoulder. I can sit with them and breathe through them until they go away.

Emotional eating can help you cope with emotions in the moment, but it's not a productive coping strategy for the long run. A key step toward breaking free from emotional eating is understanding its root cause. Write a reflection based on the following questions: Why do I eat when I'm emotional? Do I believe that eating will solve my problems?

_____

_____

_____

_____

_____

_____

_____

_____

_____

_____

_____

_____

_____

_____

_____

_____

Making Your Back Pocket List

List some mindful activities in each of these three categories of coping strategies. The next time you find yourself wanting to eat to avoid your feelings, you can choose an activity from one of these categories instead. Having this list prepared and in your back pocket can help you make healthier decisions in the moment.

Try to avoid activities that are forms of distractions like watching TV, browsing social media, and shopping. Of course, if you do end up doing so, give yourself grace! But try to take this opportunity to consciously choose mindful activities to manage your emotions.

MOVEMENT	FUN	SELF-REFLECTION
▶ Yoga	▶ Jigsaw puzzle	▶ Journaling
▶ Dance	▶ Sudoku	▶ Meditation

I am ready to manage uncomfortable emotions in a more mindful way, without turning to food or other forms of distraction.

THE HUNGER MAP

The next time you have an urge to eat to avoid your feelings, use this chart. First, ask yourself if you're hungry. If the answer is yes (even if you just ate or it's not mealtime), then eat mindfully. If the answer is no or you're not sure, then choose a mindful activity from your back pocket list (page 24). Afterward, ask yourself again if you still would like to eat. If the answer is yes, give yourself permission to eat mindfully. If the answer is no, congratulations! You just managed your emotions and prevented emotional eating.

I have the mindfulness tools I need to help me prevent emotional eating. I'm no longer afraid of facing my emotions.

Judgment can get in the way of improving your relationship with food. When it comes to food, release the "shoulds" and "shouldn'ts." Reflect on the following questions: What are some judgments I have about the way I eat? What are judgments I have about my body? What are some judgments I have about the ways other people eat?

_____

_____

_____

_____

_____

_____

_____

_____

_____

_____

_____

_____

_____

_____

_____

Unconditional Permission

Unconditional permission to eat means giving yourself full permission to eat the foods you love, without feeling that you need to work for them. The foods on the following list are neither good nor bad. Cross off any foods on the list that you cannot have due to allergies, sensitivities, or other reasons. Then, cross off the foods that you already allow yourself unconditionally. Finally, circle the foods that you don't let yourself eat or that you limit under certain conditions. Use the lines to write in foods that aren't already listed.

- potato chips
- ice cream
- chocolate
- candy
- baked goods
- bread
- potatoes

- rice
- pasta
- avocados
- vegetable oil
- fried foods
- fish
- poultry

- meat
- eggs
- nuts
- yogurt
- cheese
- fruit
- vegetables

_____

_____

_____

_____

_____

There are no good or bad foods. All foods are neutral, and I decide with my body what foods work well for me.

EAT TO YOUR HEART'S DESIRE

Give yourself unconditional permission to eat all foods. When you do this, all food becomes neutral, and no food carries the power of being overly exciting or scary. At first you might end up eating more than you thought you would, but the novelty will eventually wear off. Choose one food you circled that you'd like to eat. Release judgment and allow yourself to enjoy it. The key is to eat slowly and mindfully, bringing awareness to the flavors and your body's response.

How did it feel to eat without restriction or criticism? If you were able to eat until you were satisfied, cross this food off your list. At another time, try another food from the list. Observe your thoughts and your body's reactions throughout the process.

I release all judgments I have about food and the way I eat. I give myself unconditional permission to mindfully eat all foods I enjoy.

Discipline is a powerful tool that can help people reach their goals, but discipline when dieting can be detrimental. Ignoring your hunger, or pushing yourself when your body needs rest, can cause a disconnect between the mind and body. How do you practice discipline? How has diet-related discipline affected your relationship with food?

_____

_____

_____

_____

_____

_____

_____

_____

_____

_____

_____

_____

_____

_____

_____

_____

The Body Check-In Checklist

Get in the habit of checking in with your body throughout the day to cultivate a stronger connection between your mind and body. The more you do this, the more it will become a natural routine. Add any other questions you'd like to ask yourself in the blank spaces.

- [ ] How am I feeling?
- [ ] How is my body feeling?
- [ ] What is my pain level?
- [ ] Am I being kind to myself?
- [ ] Have I nourished my body?
- [ ] Have I given myself the rest I need?
- [ ] Have I moved my body in a way that feels good?

- [ ] What feels good to me right now?
- [ ] Am I using discipline in a healthy way?
- [ ] _____
- [ ] _____
- [ ] _____
- [ ] _____
- [ ] _____
- [ ] _____

Taking care of myself is my top priority. It's not selfish or narcissistic to attend to my needs. Compassion starts with taking care of myself first.

THE 5-MINUTE MONK

The next time you feel restless or uneasy, practice sitting with those feelings. Turn off all your devices and put them away in a drawer or somewhere not easily accessible. Tidy your area and free yourself of any distractions. Make sure you don't have any snacks nearby. Then sit, lie down, or make yourself physically comfortable.

For five minutes, sit with your emotions and observe your thoughts. If it's difficult, focus on your breathing. Get in the habit of becoming comfortable with the uncomfortable. After five minutes, go do something that you find uplifting or enjoyable.

I show myself respect through practicing compassionate discipline. Sitting with my uncomfortable emotions helps me become more self-aware. It becomes easier with practice.

Time management plays a big role in stress management. Running behind can be stressful. Are you in control of your time? How do you feel about the way you spend your time? How does your use of time affect your emotions and how you eat?

_____

_____

_____

_____

_____

_____

_____

_____

_____

_____

_____

_____

_____

_____

_____

_____

Fill My Cup First

Do you ever think about all the things you want to do but don't seem to have the time for? Let's change that. Write down what you would like to spend more time on. Put a star next to the top three things that are important to you. Write down what you would like to spend less time on. Strike through the activities that are easy to cut out or reduce.

I WANT TO SPEND MORE TIME ON . . .

creative hobbies

_____

_____

_____

_____

_____

_____

_____

I WANT TO SPEND LESS TIME ON . . .

catering to others' needs

_____

_____

_____

_____

_____

_____

_____

Practicing self-compassion and self-respect includes using my time wisely. Good time management allows me to make room for what's most important to me.

MY MINDFUL DAILY ROUTINE

Creating morning and evening routines can reduce stress and help you avoid undesirable emotions as you begin and end your day. Using the following examples as jumping off points, list three mindful activities you would like to do and write how long each will take to do. Decide on your morning and evening routines. Then, write out your schedule so you can refer to it as you commit yourself to them!

MORNING ACTIVITIES

- yoga   20 min
- journal   10 min
- breakfast   20 min
- _____
- _____

EVENING ACTIVITIES

- read   30 min
- meditate   15 min
- journal   20 min
- _____
- _____

MORNING SCHEDULE

- 7:00 am   yoga
- 7:20 am   journal
- 7:30 am   breakfast
- _____
- _____

EVENING SCHEDULE

- 9:45 pm   meditate
- 10:00 pm   read and journal
- _____
- _____

I prioritize the things that are important to me. My intention is to fill my time doing the things that help me thrive.

Eating can be enjoyed by all your senses. Observing your senses when you eat brings your awareness to your food and helps forge a more mindful connection to the eating experience. When you look at food, how does it make you feel? What makes food pleasing to your eyes? What sounds tickle your appetite?

_____

_____

_____

_____

_____

_____

_____

_____

_____

_____

_____

_____

_____

_____

_____

_____

_____

_____

Cook Up A Storm

Take a few minutes to visualize your ideal meal. It can be at your favorite restaurant, at your grandma's house, or at an imaginary place. Include details such as the table setting, dishware, decor, and the people that will join you. Will there be music playing? What will be on the menu? Who will prepare the food? What kinds of conversations will you have? How will the food smell, look, taste, and feel? What emotions arise from this experience? Now, draw your ideal meal, or describe it in words.

Food gives me energy. Food nourishes my body and soul. Food brings me joy. Food provides me comfort. I am at peace with food.

DATE NIGHT IN

Prepare a meal for you or your loved ones that is pleasing to all your senses (don't forget emotions!). Choose a recipe that makes your mouth water and pour your heart into it. Or feel free to get your favorite take-out. Take the time to make the meal look appetizing: Play with the colors, add garnishes, and use your favorite dishware. Set the table and decorate your dining area. Turn on some calming music and light some candles for ambiance if you like.

I love the way food tastes and smells. I love the way food makes me feel. I love the memories I create with food.

Media can play a significant role in the way we think and act. Persistent images on TV, in magazines, and on social media make it easy to buy into beauty standards, stereotypes, and gender roles. Negative body image can impact the way you view food, resulting in a toxic cycle of self-restriction and emotional eating. Write down and reflect on unhealthy messages you may have picked up from media. For example: I must be thin to be attractive, accepted, and loved.

Uproot the Negative Self-Talk

Negative self-talk comes from messages you've picked up from family, friends, media, and society. It manifests in rooted thoughts that repeat in your mind on a regular basis and keep you feeling "less than." List some examples of negative self-talk that affect your self-esteem. Then list your favorite affirmations that counteract these negative thoughts and repeat these empowering words each day.

Negative Self-Talk
I'm not deserving of love.
I am not attractive enough.

_____

_____

_____

_____

Favorite Affirmations
I am deserving of love exactly the way I am.
I am strong; I am attractive; I am enough.

_____

_____

_____

_____

_____

I am strong. I am smart. I am attractive. I am powerful.
I am worthy. I am loving. I am loveable. I am enough.

Being mindful means that you are focusing on one thing at a time without distraction. For example, folding laundry while watching TV isn't a bad thing, but it's not exactly "mindful." Incorporating mindful activities into your daily life can help you reduce stress and maintain your emotional balance. Reflect on the activities you do mindfully and unmindfully. How do you feel when you do something mindfully versus unmindfully?

_____

_____

_____

_____

_____

_____

_____

_____

_____

_____

_____

_____

_____

_____

_____

_____

Everyday Mindfulness

Mindfulness helps us slow down, become aware of our thoughts, relieve stress, and reduce mistakes and accidents. This allows less room for the anxiety that leads to emotional eating. Here is a list of activities that may be done mindfully. Circle the ones that you already do mindfully. Put a star next to the ones that you would like to be more mindful about.

Washing dishes

Folding laundry

Cleaning

Working

Cooking

Eating a meal

Snacking

Walking

Exercising

Journaling

Reading

Taking a shower

Brushing my teeth

Listening

I have time and will make time each day to carry out at least one task mindfully. Being mindful makes me feel _____ and _____.

MY MINDFUL V.I.T. (VERY IMPORTANT TASK)

Choose at least one activity that you starred to practice mindfully, like washing dishes. The next time you wash the dishes, do it mindfully. If you normally let the dishes pile up and do them unwillingly, shift your mindset. Get excited about scrubbing the dishes! The task at hand is going to be the most important thing you are doing in the moment. Don't rush to get it over with. Simply enjoy the process. Notice your thoughts throughout the task you've chosen. Then observe your emotions and any urge for emotional eating for the remainder of the day.

There is no task that is boring or too much trouble.
I enjoy _____. It gives me the opportunity
to be mindful and observant.

Healthy relationships are important for one's emotional well-being. Use this space to explore the following questions: What kind of relationships do I have with those around me? How do they support me? How do I support them? Are there any toxic or unsupportive relationships? How do they affect my well-being? What kind of relationships do I want to cultivate?

Support System

When you're on a wellness journey, it's important to set up a supportive environment for yourself. Make a list of people in your life that you interact with regularly, including family, coworkers, and friends. Then reflect on your relationship with each person. Are they supportive of you? Do they know about your health journey? Think about their relationship with food and how that affects you. Next to each person, write down "supportive," "neutral," or "unsupportive." Write down how you can fortify each relationship, whether by offering others your thanks or having a heart-to-heart talk.

PERSON	RELATIONSHIP

Although working on my relationship with food is hard, I know I can lean on people in my life who love and support me.

NO = YES

Set healthy boundaries with people in your life. Just because you love them, they're kind, or they need you, doesn't mean you need to spend all your time and energy on them. You must learn to manage your boundaries to protect yourself. But fear not, this can be done with grace! Learn to say no to things that threaten your ability to care for yourself or that may burden you in ways that will cause you stress or anxiety. Saying "no" in these cases is saying "yes" to yourself.

How would you like others to say no to you? How can you reflect that when you say no to them? For example, "I would love to help, but I don't think I have the capacity right now."

I fill my cup first. I take care of myself before others. I can help others with what overflows from my cup.

Holding onto a grudge is powerful—but just as powerful is forgiveness. Are you holding onto any grudges? Who or what have you not forgiven yet? How does resentment affect your mood and your daily life? How does it affect the ways you take care of yourself and nourish yourself?

_____

_____

_____

_____

_____

_____

_____

_____

_____

_____

_____

_____

_____

_____

_____

_____

_____

_____

_____

Forgive Yourself

Perhaps, like many people, you give yourself a hard time over small mistakes, or you're overly critical about your body image. In order for you to take care of yourself sustainably, I encourage you to treat yourself fairly and forgive yourself. Make a list of how you've treated yourself unkindly. Then address each item, starting with "I forgive myself for . . ."

NEGATIVE TREATMENT

1. I cut out carbs.

2. I've hated the rolls on my belly.

FORGIVENESS

1. I forgive myself for depriving myself of foods I love and need.

2. I forgive myself for being unkind to my body.

_I forgive myself for being unkind to my body. I forgive myself for the mean things I've said to myself. I forgive myself for _____ ._

HAWAIIAN-INSPIRED FORGIVENESS MEDITATION

This meditation is based on a beautiful Hawaiian prayer for forgiveness called "Ho'oponopono" (pronounced *HO oh Po no Po no*).

To begin, get into a comfortable seat or lie down and close your eyes. Relax your body and ease into your breath. Place your hands over your heart. Reflect on the things that you'd like to forgive yourself for and the people you want to forgive. For each item, recite the Ho'oponopono prayer, "I'm sorry. Please forgive me. Thank you. I love you." Then imagine releasing these thoughts into the sky. Feel the negativity lifting from your body.

I am learning to forgive those who have made me feel hurt. I am learning to forgive myself.

Connecting to nature can help you break free from the emotional eating cycle because it allows you to de-stress, restore yourself, and relax. Spending time outdoors also means less time spent on screens or engaged in unhealthy habits that can otherwise contribute to your stress and anxiety. When was the last time you connected with nature? How does your body feel when you're outdoors or connecting to nature?

Observing Nature with Wonder

Simply taking a walk, or moving as best suits your mobility, can boost your mood and help you feel grounded or inspired. Increasing these positive experiences encourages cultivation of healthy habits and reduces opportunities for emotional eating. Complete the sentences below to remind yourself of how nature can nourish you.

Nature makes me feel _____.

My favorite place in nature is _____.

My favorite smell in nature is _____.

My favorite sound in nature is _____.

My favorite animal is _____ because _____.

My favorite plant is _____ because _____.

One thing I miss about nature is _____.

What I appreciate about spring is _____.

What I appreciate about summer is _____.

What I appreciate about fall is _____.

What I appreciate about winter is _____.

Connecting with nature affects my eating by _____.

I am grateful for the earth that supports me, the sun that warms me, and the food that nourishes me.

A DAY IN THE LIFE OF AN EARTHLING

Step outside in nature to get energized. Find an outdoor space where you feel safe and comfortable, like your yard or a local park. Avoid thinking about to-dos and worries, stay present in the moment, and enjoy the outdoors.

▶ Walk barefoot on the grass or dirt.

▶ Hug a tree.

▶ Notice how the sun feels on your skin.

▶ Lie down and look for animal-shaped clouds.

▶ Watch the birds and butterflies.

▶ Take a close look at flowers and their colors.

▶ Look for a four-leaf clover.

I am living among all the beings on this earth. I receive from the earth and I give back to the earth.

Do you ever think about your mental to-do list, get overwhelmed, and end up eating instead of making progress on your tasks? If so, you are not alone. When is the last time you ate in response to feeling overwhelmed? How did it make you feel afterward?

No More Unfinished Business

What has been on your mental to-do list for ages? Having unfinished business can clutter the mind and contribute to stress, anxiety, and emotional eating. Take this opportunity to organize and systematically tackle your to-do list. Write down each task and how long each one will take. If it's not something you can do today, schedule it in your calendar. It can be something as simple as making a dentist appointment or more energy- and time-consuming like cleaning the garage or filing taxes. Compare how you feel before and after, as you cross each item off the list.

TO-DO LIST	TIME IT WILL TAKE	DATE TO BE COMPLETED

Taking just one step moves me forward. I know that as long as I look ahead, I can put one foot in front of the other.

COMB THROUGH YOUR THOUGHTS

Stream-of-consciousness journaling can help you declutter your mind, de-stress, and prevent emotional eating. Keep a journal and pen next to your bed and start writing the moment you wake up. Without overthinking, write freely without judgment or pause. You might start with your dreams or incoherent thoughts. Notice what comes up and how you feel afterward. How does it feel to start your day this way?

I am doing the best I can right now. I am proud of myself for being where I am. I am enough just the way I am.

With the rise of the digital age, there is an increasing concern about people's ability to focus and be present in the moment. If you're a digital consumer, how does your device affect you? How does it affect your emotional and mental wellness? Do you see any similar emotional or behavioral patterns between your relationship with your devices and your relationship with food?

Digital Detox Checklist

Take stock of your relationships with your devices and, for this moment, make some conscious decisions about how you will use them.

- [ ] Set timers on your phone to limit app use.
- [ ] Turn off your phone an hour before bed.
- [ ] Use an alarm clock instead of your phone.
- [ ] Keep your phone away from your bed.
- [ ] Grayscale your screen to make your phone uninteresting.
- [ ] Unfollow or mute social media accounts that make you feel bad about yourself.
- [ ] Start following accounts that inspire and support you.
- [ ] Set boundaries for your phone use and stick to them.
- [ ] Delete social media apps for a week (no need to deactivate or delete your account).

I don't need to be connected to technology to feel accepted, loved, or worthy. My life in the real world is enriching.

PLUG INTO YOURSELF

There are similarities between the ways people use digital devices and food for emotional escape. Take a few moments to observe your behavior in relation to your smartphone.

1. Set your phone far enough away so that you can't reach it without getting up.

2. Notice how often you have an urge to reach for your phone.

3. Every time you find yourself wanting to check your phone, tablet, or other device, ask yourself whether it was out of habit or to escape from your emotions.

4. Notice how this behavior compares to the urge to eat when you're not truly hungry.

Unplugging from my devices allows me to plug in to the present moment. Unplugging from social media allows me to plug in to my body and my impulses.

When it comes to food, there's a lot to be thankful for. Think about a meal you recently had. Think about the ingredients and where they came from. Who was involved in producing and cooking the food? What aspects of your meal are you grateful for?

Follow the Food Chain

Understanding the process that made it possible for you to enjoy your meals can shed new light on how you approach food.

Pick one of your favorite foods. Using your knowledge and imagination, trace the food back to its original form. Imagine each person who was involved in making it available for you.

Food Item: Potato Chips

STEP	LOCATION	PERSON INVOLVED
▶ Selling	▶ Store	▶ Cashier, bagger
▶ Transportation		▶ Truck driver

Food Item: _____

STEP	LOCATION	PERSON INVOLVED

I eat with care to honor my body. I eat with appreciation for those who make my nourishment possible.

EVERY DAY IS THANKSGIVING

The Japanese say *itadakimasu,* meaning, "I'm going to eat," before each meal. The word *gochisosama*, meaning, "Thank you for the feast," marks the end of each meal. These words express gratitude for the food and the person who prepared the meal. Pausing to express gratitude before and after a meal allows for a mindful eating experience.

Come up with a word or phrase of gratitude to mark the beginning and the end of your meals. Use this word or phrase, at every meal. Even a simple silent, "Thank you," can be enough.

I'm grateful for the abundance of food that is accessible to me. I'm grateful that nourishing my body is a pleasurable experience.

Overcoming emotional eating doesn't happen overnight. Along with practice, it requires patience, trust, and self-compassion. Reflect on the following questions: How am I treating myself through this process of improving my relationship with food? How can I be more compassionate with myself? How can I celebrate myself for stepping into this work?

Self-Compassion Exercise

Complete each sentence below to remind yourself of how much love you deserve!

▶ I am most proud of myself for _____.

▶ One thing I love about myself is _____.

▶ I am currently working on _____.

▶ One hard thing I've overcome is _____.

▶ I want to take care of myself because _____.

▶ My biggest strength is _____.

▶ I celebrate myself by _____.

▶ I want to forgive myself for _____.

▶ I want to accept myself for _____.

▶ I want to love myself for _____.

▶ One thing that would make me truly happy is _____.

▶ I can practice self-compassion by _____.

▶ I promise that I will _____.

▶ I will take care of my body by _____.

I choose to love myself. I choose to be kind to myself.
I choose to give myself grace. I choose to trust myself.

TAKE A PERSONAL JOY DAY

Take a full day, half-day, or even an hour for yourself alone. Choose something that you want to do purely for pleasure. It might be taking a restorative yoga class, or baking cookies and watching a movie. Drop any feelings of guilt about losing productivity, being selfish, or doing something for your own satisfaction. This intentional practice is about showing up for yourself and having fun. If you can't do it today, block out time in your calendar this week for yourself.

I deserve to feel pure joy. I deserve to be happy. I deserve to treat myself. I deserve to love myself unconditionally. I deserve to be me.

Showing self-respect means showing up for yourself and unapologetically taking up space. It also means protecting your boundaries. Ask yourself: When do I act small or hide? Do I have healthy boundaries? How does the way I respect or disrespect myself relate to how I eat and perceive my body?

_____

_____

_____

_____

_____

_____

_____

_____

_____

_____

_____

_____

_____

_____

_____

_____

_____

_____

_____

Show Up for Yourself

Circle all the answers that apply. Write in any additional answers that apply to you.

I will practice taking up space by . . .
 Voicing my opinion and concerns.
 Wearing clothes that express who I am.
 Taking as much physical space and time as I need.

_____

I will practice healthy boundaries by . . .
 Establishing a reasonable work-life balance.
 Saying no to what doesn't serve me.
 Saying no to what is beyond my capacity.
 Respecting my time through time management.
 Releasing toxic relationships.

_____

I will honor my health by . . .
 Eating the foods that nourish me.
 Moving my body in a way that feels joyful.
 Expressing gratitude for my body.

_____

I practice self-care by honoring my needs. I practice self-care by setting healthy boundaries. I practice self-care by letting go of what doesn't serve me.

TAKE UP YOUR SPACE

Imagine you're at a party in a room full of people. Your friends, family, and loved ones are present. You also see your colleagues, your boss, and even some new faces. People are coming up to you. Who are they? What do they say? Notice your reactions. Remember that you're working on self-respect. How will you respond? What are their reactions to your response? Continue to imagine your interactions with different people in the room. How will you physically move through the room? How will you take up space? What does it feel like to own your space unapologetically in this moment?

I deserve to take up as much space as I need. I deserve to fully express myself. I deserve to be respected.

As you work on improving your relationship with food and over-coming emotional eating, it is likely that there will be times when you just want to eat in response to your emotions. If you have an emotional eating episode, write out how you feel in the moments afterward. What led to this episode of emotional eating? What have you learned?

_____

_____

_____

_____

_____

_____

_____

_____

_____

_____

_____

_____

_____

_____

_____

_____

_____

Catch and Release

You may find yourself feeling many different emotions after an emotional eating episode. In this exercise, you'll identify these emotions and consciously let them go.

Circle the feelings you are experiencing that you would like to release:

ASHAMED   OUT OF CONTROL   EMBARRASSED

GUILTY   FRUSTRATED   ANGRY

ANXIOUS   NEUTRAL   DISAPPOINTED

STRESSED   THE NEED TO   _____

POWERLESS   EXERCISE   _____

Now, circle how you would like to feel instead, after eating:

JOYFUL   FREE   CONFIDENT

SATISFIED   GRATEFUL   CONTENT

COMFORTABLE   CONNECTED   AT PEACE

GROUNDED   ADEQUATE   _____

TRUSTING   SAFE   _____

I am free. I am calm. I am confident.
I am free. I am safe. I am inspired.
I am free. I am joyful. I am adequate.

BALLOON RELEASE MEDITATION

First, review the feelings you listed in the Catch and Release exercise (page 68). Then, close your eyes and soften your breath. Scan your body for any areas of tension, as you may be subconsciously storing emotions in your body. Imagine each emotion in its own helium-filled balloon and hold them out in front of you.

Take one balloon at a time and acknowledge the emotion in the balloon. Tell yourself that there is no reason for you to hold onto it. Release the emotion by letting the balloon go and watching it float away. How do you feel? Repeat the process for each of the emotions you want to release.

I know that I have everything I need. I must release what hurts me and keeps me small. I let go and surrender.

Do you ever continue to eat even when your stomach is full and then end up feeling bad? What goes on in your mind when you eat beyond fullness? How do you determine what is "too much" food? How do you know when you've had the right amount of food?

_____

_____

_____

_____

_____

_____

_____

_____

_____

_____

_____

_____

_____

_____

_____

_____

_____

_____

Watch Your Language

When you say, "I overate," or "I ate too much," do you use these phrases to mean that you've eaten past a comfortable level of fullness? Or are you being critical about the amount of food you've eaten?

Write down the thoughts that fill your mind, then rewrite them so that they become objective statements.

CURRENT LANGUAGE	NEW LANGUAGE
▶ I ate too much.	▶ I ate past fullness
▶ Why did I eat so much?	▶ That meal was so delicious, I ate more than I normally do. And that's okay.

I choose to love myself no matter how much I've eaten.
I choose to accept my imperfect journey to improve my
relationship with food.

SEATED CAT-COW POSE

Generally speaking, yoga is best done a few hours after your last meal. But here's one gentle pose to try after eating past fullness. Use it as a way to soothe yourself and slow any resulting negative, critical, or judgmental feelings.

Sit on the floor with your legs crossed or on a chair with your feet on the floor. Sit up tall and place your hands on your knees. As you inhale through your nose, open your chest, arch your back slightly and look upward. Then, as you exhale through your nose, lower your chin to your chest and round your back. Repeat this several times slowly, moving with your breath.

The food I consume becomes energy I need. I trust my body to digest the food and to deliver nutrients where they need to go.

All too often, the definition of health is oversimplified and reduced to numbers and appearances: clothing size, numbers on a scale, calories, and step count. But a big part of being in good health involves emotions and stress levels. Take a step back and redefine health. What does "healthy" mean to you? Consider your physical, emotional, and mental health.

Health Beyond Numbers

It's easy to lose sight of the big picture when it comes to good health. It's important to embrace how you feel intrinsically and within your body. Circle the statements that focus on qualitative health measures, rather than quantitative ones (that focus on numbers and specifics).

Moving my body helps boost my mood.

I aim to consume five servings of fruits and vegetables daily.

I rest my body when I'm tired.

I need to lose ten pounds for my health.

Having a mid-afternoon snack gives me the energy I need.

I eat when I'm hungry and stop eating when I'm comfortably full.

Now, add some of your own health markers that don't rely on numbers:

_____

_____

_____

_____

_____

_____

I let go of the need to be a certain size. I let go of the desire to look a certain way.

VISUALIZE YOUR BEST HEALTH

Imagine yourself at your best health, whatever that means to you. Instead of visualizing what you look like, think about how you would feel. What are you capable of? How does it feel? How strong are you? How happy are you? Do you feel supported by friends and loved ones? What hobbies do you have? What relationships do you have with food and your body? What activities do you participate in? What kinds of conversations do you have? What do you have the energy for? Write or draw what comes up for you.

Healthy means I can do the things I love. Healthy means I can laugh from my heart. Healthy means I can eat my favorite foods.

Many people grew up with the notion that certain foods (ice cream, pizza, candy, etc.) were "treats" to be enjoyed as part of a celebration or after a job well done. This sends a message that you can only eat those food if you deserve them. Ask yourself: When am I deserving of indulging in "treats?" Do I punish myself when I eat something "bad"?

_____

_____

_____

_____

_____

_____

_____

_____

_____

_____

_____

_____

_____

_____

_____

_____

Celebrate Anew

For many people, the go-to way to celebrate events or large and small accomplishments is with food. Often, the foods chosen for celebrations are considered treats or indulgences, which can trigger a complicated dynamic with these foods. While you are working on improving your relationship with food and treating all foods as neutral, it can be helpful to find ways to celebrate that don't involve food.

List what you would like to celebrate, no matter how small or seemingly insignificant:

_____

_____

_____

_____

Brainstorm mindful ways to celebrate that don't involve food, such as sharing the news with a friend or watching your favorite film:

_____

_____

_____

_____

Go ahead and celebrate!

I allow myself to eat my favorite foods any time. I don't need to prove that I am worthy of eating something I enjoy.

JOYFUL MOVEMENT

Many people use exercise as a means to lose weight or to punish themselves when they feel bad about their eating, but it's critical to remember that exercise is an effective way to reduce stress and manage negative emotions. The next time you exercise, disassociate it from burning calories, losing weight, and self-imposed punishment. Instead, relish the exercise you do because it increases endorphins, boosts your mood, gets your blood flowing, and lowers stress. Note that these benefits are all unrelated to food and body image.

1. Choose a movement that you enjoy.

2. Set an intention that's not related to weight or guilt. For example, "Today I'm going to move my body to release stress," or, "I'm going to stretch to relieve back pain."

3. Check in with your body during your chosen movement.

4. Thank your body for what it is capable of.

I'm grateful for this body, which is a vessel that carries me. I respect my body by moving with joy. I respect my body by letting it rest.

There are different ways to deal with stress: You can push through it, numb yourself to it intentionally (by doing things like watching television and eating snacks), or release it mindfully. What are some ways you cope with stress and emotions besides food? Which ways are effective? Think about short-term and long-term effects.

_____

_____

_____

_____

_____

_____

_____

_____

_____

_____

_____

_____

_____

_____

_____

_____

_____

Mindful Mandala

Mandalas are beautifully decorated circles used in meditation and relaxation. Coloring mandalas can be a mindful activity that incorporates repetitive movement, creativity, and focus.

If you are feeling stressed and the urge to eat is a distraction, try coloring in this mandala as a gentle way to slow down and come into the present moment.

Use your choice of artistic tools (crayons, pencils, markers) to make your mandala come to life. Take your time and enjoy the process. Notice how you feel as you are coloring and any thoughts that arise.

Compare how you feel before and after the activity. Do you feel any calmer? Do you feel more connected to your breath, your body, or your emotions? How does your stress level compare once you have finished coloring the mandala in your chosen way?

I don't have anything to stress about. I don't have anything to worry about. I don't have anything to be upset about. Everything is okay.

RESTORE AND REFRESH

Restorative yoga poses don't require contorting your body and are passive and relaxing. Here's a pose that will help you relax by activating the parasympathetic nervous system, or the "rest and digest" response. The more opportunities you have to feel calm, the less you will be tempted to engage in emotional eating.

Lie down facing upward. Bend your knees, open your hips, and put the soles of your feet together. Place a pillow underneath each leg so each limb is completely supported. Bring your hands out to the sides of your body with your palms facing up. Close your eyes, soften your breath, and relax. Stay in this pose for 5 to 10 minutes.

I allow myself to relax and let go. By focusing on breathing and resting, I am learning to care for my mind and body.

Work and daily stress can make it tempting to snack endlessly or skip lunch. Do you find yourself eating lunch at your desk? Do you snack mindlessly as you work on your latest project, or in your car between appointments? How do you manage eating as you work, study, or go about your everyday tasks?

Work-Lunch Balance Checklist

Being conscious and respectful of your body and how you nourish it is an everyday experience. Take stock of this at your next lunch break, using the following strategies.

RESPECT YOUR TIME

☐ Set aside 30 to 60 minutes for lunch every workday.

☐ Block out your calendar to prevent meetings being scheduled at your lunchtime.

☐ Eat lunch at a designated area that's not your workspace.

☐ If you must eat at your desk, shut down your computer and clear your desk.

☐ Take breaks and fuel yourself with healthy snacks you enjoy. This can prevent snacking mindlessly as you work.

☐ _____

☐ _____

BE PREPARED

☐ Plan your meals ahead of time.

☐ Have snacks available so you don't become famished.

☐ Keep a stress relief activity nearby.

☐ _____

☐ _____

I won't let work get in the way of my self-care. I choose to take care of my body first and foremost.

YOGA BREAK

Looking for a quick and mindful way to relax instead of snacking?

Here's a 5-minute yoga sequence you can do in a chair. Feel free to return to this mini-break in moments when you're feeling stressed, overwhelmed, or otherwise emotionally elevated.

1. Sit up at the edge of your seat with your feet on the floor.

2. Close your eyes and take a deep breath.

3. Relax your shoulders and roll them back a few times.

4. Lift your arms overhead and stretch.

5. Bring your arms out to the sides like a cactus.

6. Turn your neck slowly from side to side

7. Rest your arms down at your sides.

8. Pick up one foot and cross your ankle over the other thigh. Return to your starting position, then repeat on the other side.

I always make time for self-care because it's important to me. I am never too busy to breathe and move my body.

The holidays bring forth different feelings for each person. Perhaps you experience excitement, joy, stress, loneliness, indifference, or a combination of emotions. Reflect on the feelings you experience during holidays. How is your eating affected? How would you like to feel at these times?

_____

_____

_____

_____

_____

_____

_____

_____

_____

_____

_____

_____

_____

_____

_____

_____

_____

_____

Set Your Holiday Intentions

The holidays often center around large quantities of food. For some reason, the feasts at gatherings often could feed five times the number of people present, which means lots of food to eat, whether you're hungry or not. It's important to set intentions for the holidays in order to stay grounded and avoid eating more than your body desires.

How do you want to feel during the holiday season? What can you let go of this year? How can you honor your body? Create a list of intentions:

INTENTIONS

I don't have to eat all the food that's available.

I won't participate in diet conversations.

The holiday season is about enjoying time with loved ones. I choose not to stress or worry. I choose to stay grounded in my body.

MINDFUL EATING: HOLIDAY EDITION

You may be used to feeling uncomfortably full by the end of a holiday meal. The next time you attend a holiday event, try to eat mindfully. Consider the following before you begin your meal.

1. How hungry am I?

2. If you are in a self-serve scenario, survey all of the food before serving yourself. Choose the foods that are most inviting to you. You can always go back for more.

3. Try to eat slowly, placing your utensils down between bites.

4. If you plan to enjoy dessert, consider stopping before you are full.

5. It's okay to say no thank you to more food.

Attending a holiday meal doesn't mean I need to eat more than I can handle. I will enjoy the delicious food and eat until I'm satisfied.

As we transition from childhood to adolescence and adulthood, it's not uncommon to lose touch with intuition. We get in our heads and follow rules to make sure we're on the right track or to be accepted. In what kinds of situations do you feel that you have to make an effort to stay within socially accepted boundaries? How does this make you feel? Are you aware of how your body reacts? When can you loosen up?

_____

_____

_____

_____

_____

_____

_____

_____

_____

_____

_____

_____

_____

_____

_____

Color the Sun Purple

It can feel constricting to be confined by standards that have been engrained in us since childhood. Take this opportunity to question rules and guidelines. In the space below, draw a sun of your choosing. Now, get ready to color it. Here's the catch: Let go of your image of how the picture *should* look. You're allowed to color outside the lines, color the sun purple, and do whatever you want. Get creative. It doesn't have to look pretty. This isn't for anyone's eyes but your own. When you're done, reflect on the process. How did it feel to release rules? How does this exercise relate to how you think you should eat and how you feel your body should look?

There are rules that we must follow and rules that we can break. I release the rules that don't serve me and that keep me confined.

INTUITIVE ART

Intuitive eating is a mindful approach to nourishing your body. Intuitive art, or creative practice, is another way to nurture yourself that doesn't involve eating or drinking. Choose something you'd like to try doing, as a mindful way to explore your body and mind. This is an intuitive practice; you don't need mastery or skills to do it.

DANCE: Pick a song and move the way your body wants. Make up your own dance moves!

DRAW: Pick up a marker and move it across the paper spontaneously. You can even close your eyes and draw. You may be surprised by what you end up with!

WRITE: Write a story or a poem. Don't worry about grammar, punctuation, or any typical "rules."

Don't worry about the end result. Focus on your enjoyment of the activity in the moment.

I'm not concerned about the result. What's important is that I'm true to myself. I'm tuning in to my intuition and enjoying the process.

It's completely normal to feel overwhelmed by the thought of overcoming emotional eating. But imagine for a moment what life would be like without emotional eating. Use the space below to write about how it would feel to no longer eat because of your feelings. Imagine how your life would be different.

_____

_____

_____

_____

_____

_____

_____

_____

_____

_____

_____

_____

_____

_____

_____

_____

_____

_____

Through a Holistic Lens

Because everything is interconnected, we cannot treat emotional eating as an isolated challenge.

Reflect on how each category of your life is affected, directly and indirectly, by your relationship with food.

FAMILY (When I'm stressed about eating, I'm not emotionally available.)

_____

_____

WORK (I'm unfocused when I worry about being judged for my size.)

_____

_____

SOCIAL LIFE (I fear what others think of me when I eat.)

_____

_____

HEALTH & WELLNESS (I'm delaying health appointments until my eating is controlled.)

_____

_____

Food gives me energy to move my body, fuels my brain, and keeps me strong. I have a healthy relationship with food.

DREAMS COME TRUE

Imagine your ideal life five to ten years into the future. Start with the moment you wake up. How are you feeling? Look around and see what your room looks like. Decide how you will start your day. Imagine how you move through the day. Notice the people in your life. Listen to the conversations you're having with them. How are you showing up for yourself? Imagine your meals. How do they taste? How is your relationship with food and with your body? Notice how you feel at the end of the day when you go to bed.

I can achieve all of my dreams and goals. My dream life is free from food rules, diet culture, and negative body image.

Distorted relationships with food and the body often start in childhood and remain through adulthood. Think about who and what has influenced you: caretakers, schoolteachers, peers, television, magazines, social media, diet trends. Then think about your answers to the following questions: Growing up, what was my relationship with food? What was my relationship with my body? What influences remain till this day?

Food History Assessment

In this exercise, you'll examine where you picked up your beliefs and behavioral patterns related to food. You'll explore which of these continue to influence your eating habits and patterns today. Be on the lookout for beliefs and behaviors that are deeply ingrained in you.

What were some fad diets that you tried?

What were the short-term and long-term outcomes? Include both physical and mental outcomes.

Growing up, did you have rules about food? Were certain foods restricted?

Did you ever fear there wouldn't be enough food? Why?

What foods were considered good and bad?

How did your caretakers speak of their relationship with food and with their body?

How does your relationship with food growing up affect how you eat today?

I am no longer bound by food rules. I am no longer influenced by diet culture. I trust my body. I trust myself to eat.

TOSS IT OUT

Did you know that you can literally throw away your unwanted thoughts? This surprisingly simple yet effective ability comes in handy, especially when you're confronting your own negative self-talk around eating.

1. On a loose sheet of paper, write down any negative thoughts, rules, and messages you have about food and your body that you want to release. For example, "I must lose weight to be attractive," or "I am ashamed of eating so much."

2. Rip up the paper.

3. Throw away the pieces in the trash or recycle bin. Notice how you feel as you release these unwelcome messages.

4. Repeat as needed.

I fill my mind with healthy thoughts that lift me up.
I release all negative thoughts that bring me down.

Anxiety, a common trigger for emotional eating, is a natural response to stress and uncertainty. But if left untended, anxiety can negatively affect your daily life. Instead of avoiding your anxiety and letting it potentially lead to emotional eating, examine it and find ways to mindfully appease yourself. Write down what makes you feel anxious. What symptoms do you experience? How do you cope with anxiety?

_____

_____

_____

_____

_____

_____

_____

_____

_____

_____

_____

_____

_____

_____

_____

_____

The 5-4-3-2-1 Technique

Anxiety can be triggered by worrying about the future or being stuck in the past. Mindfulness can help you feel calm and consequently prevent emotional eating. It's a good idea to have a few mindful techniques ready to use when anxiety strikes. For example, when you become anxious or unsettled, try this exercise to stay in the present.

Five things that you can see

1. _____

2. _____

3. _____

4. _____

5. _____

Four things that you can touch

1. _____

2. _____

3. _____

4. _____

(continued)

The 5-4-3-2-1 Technique *(continued)*

Three things that you can hear

1. _____

2. _____

3. _____

Two things that you can smell

1. _____

2. _____

One thing you can taste

1. _____

Observe your thoughts and feelings. How is your anxiety level now? Do you feel calmer, more centered, or more present in the moment?

I choose to focus on the present moment. Everything I need is here with me now. I release the past.

YOU ARE SUPPORTED

Lie down on a yoga mat or on the floor with your arms out to the sides and your legs apart. Close your eyes and connect to your breath. Take a few clearing breaths and come back to natural breathing. Scan your body and release any tension you are holding onto. Then, bring your awareness to the entire back side of your body that is in contact with the floor beneath you.

Acknowledge the immensity of the land you live on. Then feel with your body that you are fully supported by the earth beneath you. Bring your awareness to the front side of your body. Feel the lightness and freedom of the air on your skin. Know that you are fully supported in every aspect of your life.

I am supported by the earth beneath me. I am taken care of by the sky above me. I am safe. I am fully supported.

If you're like most people who procure their food from grocery store shelves, you likely don't think twice about where your food comes from. This can contribute to the lack of attention and awareness related to what you're putting into your body. On the other hand, being connected to how food is grown can inspire more mindful ways of eating and discourage emotional eating. How often are you conscious of where your food comes from? Think about things like meats and processed foods in particular.

Food Wisdom

Take a few minutes to gain some wisdom about the foods that nourish your body. This can help close the gap between you and the source of your food.

Choose a favorite fruit or vegetable that has a growing process you're unfamiliar with, like okra, artichokes, kiwi, or another favorite that sparks your curiosity!

Then, commit yourself to some *fun* research and draw or describe each of these characteristics:

Name of the fruit/vegetable: _____

What does the plant look like? _____

What does the flower look like? _____

Where is it grown? _____

Where did it originate? _____

When is it in season? _____

How long does it take from planting to harvest? _____

I'm curious about the wisdom hidden in the pulp of a sweet tangerine. I'm curious about the secrets of the soil that nurtures bright red beets.

GREET YOUR GREEN THUMB

When's the last time you watched a plant grow? Growing vegetables can help decrease stress and bring greater awareness to your relationship with food. You don't even have to get your hands dirty.

Start by growing a vegetable from scraps, indoors or outdoors: Place a carrot top, the base of a celery stalk, or the base of a head of lettuce in a dish with an inch of water. Keep it near a window for sunlight and change the water every couple of days. Watch how it grows in a matter of days!

Deepening my connection to the natural world of fruits and vegetables inspires me to deepen my connection to my mind, body, and soul.

Your relationship with food can change shape in the presence of others. Reflect on how your eating behaviors are different when you are with other people. Do you normally eat alone or with others? When you are with others, do you eat different foods? Do you tend to feel self-conscious, or are you able to enjoy meals comfortably with other people around?

Listen to Your Body Talk

Conversations can make or break your relationship with food and your body so it's important to be mindful and create a healthy support system for yourself through how you talk about bodies with others.

Write down conversation topics you focus on with others regarding food and the body.

_____

_____

_____

_____

_____

If the conversations are unhealthy, how can they be gentler and more accepting?

For example, "tips for losing weight" could instead focus on how listening to the body can be a positive step toward good health.

_____

_____

_____

_____

_____

I am in control of how I perceive my body. I am in control of how I speak of my body.

MINDFUL EATING BUDDY

Invite someone to enjoy a mindful meal with you. This is a wonderful way to create a support system as you work on breaking free from emotional eating. Explain to your buddy the benefits and how to accomplish mindful eating (page 6).

Benefits of mindful eating:

▶ Finding joy in eating

▶ Listening to the body's signals for hunger and fullness

▶ Eating the amount that feels best for your body

▶ _____

▶ _____

▶ _____

After the meal, ask your buddy about their experience. Then ask yourself how it was different eating mindfully with someone versus eating alone.

Eating can be simple. Eating can be comfortable. Eating can by pleasurable. Eating can be a joyful experience to share with friends and loved ones.

Learning to become aware of your digestion is essential for connecting with your body and eating optimally. Think about your answers to the following questions: Am I in tune with my digestive system? How does my body react to different foods? How does my stomach handle spicy foods? Oily foods? Raw foods? Cooked foods?

Digestion Checklist

Being aware of your digestive system will help you respond to your body and give it what it needs—whether it's the right nourishment, rest, or extra attention.

Go through the assessment below and mark what applies to you. You can also write in your own ideas for staying aware of your digestion. This exercise is not meant to self-diagnose any ailments, but to help you become more aware of your body so you can make healthy choices.

☐ I chew my food thoroughly.

☐ I usually eat until I'm comfortably full.

☐ I am aware of specific foods that don't agree with my gut.

☐ My bowel movements are regular.

☐ I'm aware of the conditions of my stool.

☐ _____

☐ _____

☐ _____

Eating isn't about calories in and calories out. My whole body comes together to ensure that food is digested, toxins are filtered, and nutrients are absorbed.

A SOOTHING ABDOMINAL MASSAGE

If you need some help with gut motility (perhaps if you notice you're feeling a bit backed up), try this simple massage at any time.

Start in a hero pose: Kneel on the floor or a mat, then move your feet slightly apart so you can sit between your feet. If you have sensitive knees, you can simply sit in a chair. Make fists with both hands and place them on your legs where they meet your abdominal area. Then fold your torso forward over your fists. Gently roll your fists against your abdomen in a circular motion a few times. Breathe deeply as you do this. Then roll your fists in the opposite direction. Come up slowly.

Take note; how do you feel now?

I thank my body for keeping me well. I thank my body for telling me what it needs. I thank my body for staying strong.

In a goal-driven society, it's all too easy to push self-care aside. Do you ever feel that enjoying a meal, taking a nap, or doing something nice for yourself is taking time away from what's more important? Do you base your self-worth on productivity? What do you prioritize over self-care?

_____

_____

_____

_____

_____

_____

_____

_____

_____

_____

_____

_____

_____

_____

_____

_____

_____

_____

Writing Your Timeline

Do you ever feel as if you're in a hamster wheel and not accomplishing enough at work, at school, socially, or at home? Does the accumulated frustration contribute to emotional eating? If you can feel at peace with where you are in your life, you will have more room to take care of your needs and prevent emotional eating.

Use the timeline below to write in your milestones and accomplishments. Accomplishments include setting boundaries, finding purpose, and starting your journey to heal your relationship with food.

How does it feel to see your life in this perspective?

I am exactly where I need to be. I have time to take care of my mind, body, and heart.

WRITE YOUR LEGACY

It can be easy to get caught up in the challenges of the day-to-day and find yourself snacking or grazing on foods for comfort. Taking a step back to reflect on who you are and having a clear vision of yourself can free you from daily frustrations and consequent emotional eating.

Focusing on what's most important to you, answer below in third person as if you're describing your legacy.

1. Briefly summarize your life. _____

_____

2. What are you remembered for? _____

_____

3. What are your values? _____   _____

_____

4. How do you make others feel? _____

_____

5. What fulfills you? _____

_____

Rewrite a polished version so you can read this aloud to yourself every day to help you feel aligned and grounded.

I follow my heart so I can feel joy. I follow my guiding north star so I can be free.

Emotional eating can lead to negative feelings about your health and body image. How do you perceive your body? When do these thoughts become louder? Are they more noticeable when you're getting dressed or at the beach? How does your view of your body affect the way you eat? Do you compare your body to other people's?

_____

_____

_____

_____

_____

_____

_____

_____

_____

_____

_____

_____

_____

_____

_____

_____

Body Image Checklist

Use this checklist to become aware of what contributes to the perception of your body and how to maintain a healthy outlook. The goal is to be able to accept your body the way it is.

Social Comparison

- [ ] Stop following social media accounts that promote dieting and weight loss.
- [ ] Stop comparing yourself to other people on social media, television, etc.
- [ ] Stop comparing your body to those of others.
- [ ] _____
- [ ] _____

Wardrobe

- [ ] Sort your clothes into comfortable and not so comfortable.
- [ ] Get rid of clothes that aren't comfortable.
- [ ] Don't purchase clothes that aren't completely comfortable.
- [ ] When trying on clothes, check for comfort first before looking in the mirror to see how the item looks on you.
- [ ] _____
- [ ] _____

My worth is not determined by my clothing size. My worth cannot be measured by the shape of my body.

SEND YOUR BODY LOVE

Lie down on your back and close your eyes. Take a few breaths to relax your mind and body. Imagine the sun directly above you and feel the rays warming your skin. Let the energy of the sun radiate throughout your body and gather at your center. Then, imagine the light moving down your arms and out through your palms. Place your palms gently on your body, starting from your head. Send it loving energy from your hands. Receive the energy and notice how it feels. Continue this process with the rest of your body.

I love my body unconditionally. It is perfect the way it is now. I choose not to let anyone else decide how my body should look.

When you have a strong mind-body connection, it becomes second nature to give your body what it needs. This means giving your body rest when it's tired, turning to mindful activities when you're stressed, and eating foods you enjoy in the optimal amounts for you. Becoming in tune with your body's signals takes practice but can reward you with less anxiety about food. What messages are you receiving from your body right now? What does it need? What would it appreciate?

Tuning in to Your Sensations

Practice connecting to your body by observing sensations. Close communication is helpful to be in tune with hunger and fullness cues.

Close your eyes and take a few breaths. Then tune in to your body.

Describe how your body is feeling regarding each of these different points of awareness:

► Temperature (Am I warm, cool, comfortable?)

► Breath (Is my breath smooth, short, fast, harsh?)

► Pain and tightness (What are the sensations?)

► Energy level (What's my internal battery percentage?)

► Thirst (Am I adequately hydrated?)

How is each area of your body feeling right now?

Take a moment with each body part. It's completely fine if you don't feel anything out of the norm.

► Head   ► Abdomen

► Eyes   ► Back

► Mouth   ► Hips

► Throat   ► Fingertips

► Chest   ► _____

I am aware of the physical sensations of my body. I am in touch with the messages from my body. I am in tune with my body's needs.

IN A HEARTBEAT

Find a quiet place so that you can connect with subtle sensations in your body. First, focus on the sounds around you. Then bring your awareness within. Notice your breath and pay attention to its rhythm. Observe how your chest and abdomen expand and return with each breath. Now move on to your heartbeat. Start by placing your hand over your heart. Once you're able to feel your heartbeat, remove your hand and see if you can still feel it.

I trust my body to tell me what I need. I trust my body to tell me what I desire. I trust in my body.

All too often in our culture, busy-ness is seen as a sign of "success." It's no wonder that it can be difficult to find time to sit down for a meal. What is *your* definition of success? Do you associate being busy with success? Do you ever multitask due to internal or external pressure? What gets sent to the backburner of your life and how can you reset your priorities?

_____

_____

_____

_____

_____

_____

_____

_____

_____

_____

_____

_____

_____

_____

_____

_____

_____

The Multitasker

The effectiveness of multitasking has been questioned since
1995 when a study in the *Journal of Experimental Psychology* found
that switching back and forth between cognitive tasks slows down
productivity. And yet, multitasking is so pervasive that people often
don't even realize they're doing it, though they may feel the effects
of multitasking, such as inability to focus, increased impulsivity,
increased anxiety, and a decline in overall health. Emotional eating
can, at times, take the form of multitasking—for example, when you
eat mindlessly while working or watching television. As a result, you
will likely consume significantly more food and feel less satisfied
when multitasking than when you eat mindfully.

To curb the impulse to multitask, try this exercise to see if you
can fully concentrate on multiple tasks simultaneously:

Write the alphabet backward from Z to A while paying full attention to the sounds around you.

How did you do? If it was difficult to carry out a task and tune
in to just one of your senses, think about how much you are able to
pay attention to tasting your food and monitoring your satiety when
eating while you work.

*I have the time to complete one task at a time. I am at my
best when I am present with each task.*

MINDFUL MEDITATION

Now that you know how difficult it is to truly multitask, practice paying close attention to something you perhaps normally do without focus: walking. If you have limited mobility, consider another thing you do regularly without focus, like breathing, smelling something, tapping your fingers, or another activity.

Try this meditation for 5 to 10 minutes, adapting it to your body and mobility needs.

1. Find a clear path, even if it's in your bedroom (you can walk back and forth).

2. Slowly, take one step at a time so you're aware as you put one foot down and lift the other.

3. Notice how your body feels as you walk.

4. Pay attention to all your senses.

   How was this experience similar to mindful eating?

I am aware of every movement of my limbs. I am aware of every muscle and bone. I am aware of every shift in my body.

With the overwhelming amount of conflicting nutritional information out in the world, it's easy to forget to enjoy your food. Use the space below to describe the last time you ate for pleasure. Then describe a time when you ate a food that you don't enjoy simply because you felt it was healthy.

_____

_____

_____

_____

_____

_____

_____

_____

_____

_____

_____

_____

_____

_____

_____

_____

_____

_____

Reconnect to the Joy of Eating

Emotional eating can happen as a result of dieting and restricting yourself. Eating foods that aren't satisfying can also lead to emotional eating. In this exercise, connect to the joy of eating by listening to your body's needs and seeking satisfaction.

List eight foods you ate recently, then rate how satisfied you were with each. A score of 0 is very unsatisfied and 10 is very satisfied. If you rate any foods below a 6, write down why you ate it. Was it because you prioritized health over enjoyment? Notice any patterns related to how you choose the foods you eat.

FOOD ITEM	SATISFACTION RATING	EXPLANATION (SCORE <6)
1. _____	_____	_____
2. _____	_____	_____
3. _____	_____	_____
4. _____	_____	_____
5. _____	_____	_____
6. _____	_____	_____
7. _____	_____	_____
8. _____	_____	_____

I eat with joy and satisfaction. I am in control of how I fuel my body. I focus on joy as the nourishment I need.

SATISFACTION OVER JUDGMENT

Choose a food that you know will satisfy you. Let go of any judgment you have about eating it. Ask yourself if your body would accept it. If you think it will, indulge mindfully and release guilt. Focus on satisfaction.

If you believe that your body will react negatively, can you come up with an alternative item that will satisfy you? For example, perhaps you're lactose intolerant and, though you love ice cream, you know it won't agree with you. You may decide to have coconut milk ice cream because both you and your stomach would be satisfied.

Pleasure is an important part of my health. I take pleasure in eating foods that satisfy both my stomach and my palate.

Emotional eating can be a way to avoid your fears, such as:

▶ Fear of dealing with discomfort

▶ Fear of facing the unknown

▶ Fear of being rejected

▶ Fear of taking up too much space

Write down some of your fears and explain how they impact the way you eat and take care of your body.

_____

_____

_____

_____

_____

_____

_____

_____

_____

_____

_____

_____

_____

_____

Delving into Personal Matters

Choose an unresolved issue you've been avoiding that contributes to your emotional eating. Perhaps it's an uncomfortable conversation about setting your boundaries with someone. Use this exercise to sort it out.

Unresolved issue: _____

This affects me emotionally by _____.

This affects me physically by _____.

I have been avoiding this because _____.

If I were to resolve this, it would make me feel _____.

If I were to resolve this, I would have room for _____.

What do I have to lose? _____

Steps to resolve this issue:

1. _____

2. _____

3. _____

I am capable of overcoming my fears and challenges.
I have the confidence to step outside my comfort zone.
Challenges are opportunities for growth.

There are things we must do in life—like paying bills and doing the laundry—that we don't love and that can add to our daily stresses and lead to emotional eating. What are some of your least favorite activities?

What types of emotions arise in relation to these activities? What are your tendencies when you're feeling resistant? Do you engage in emotional eating?

Shifting Perspectives

Sometimes all it takes is a shift in perspective to make chores and responsibilities less stressful. Being truly appreciative of these tasks can lessen the stresses that result in emotional eating.

List five of your least favorite activities. Then write why you are grateful for each. Take your gratitude a step or two further than you normally would.

ACTIVITY	GRATITUDE
Paying bills.	I'm grateful for the electricity to cook, heat my home, provide light, and charge my devices. I wouldn't be able to fulfill my basic needs without electricity.

Notice how gratitude helps lighten the load of day-to-day chores and tasks.

All it takes is a shift in perspective for me to see the beauty in mundane tasks.

MAKE IT FUN

Make your least favorite activity the highlight of your day and save yourself from emotional eating.

Prepare by making the ideal playlist. If you need to concentrate, look for soothing background sounds or classical music. If the task doesn't require you to think, play upbeat music or your favorite blast from the past. To motivate yourself, decide on a fun, non-food reward for when you've completed the task. It doesn't have to cost a penny. Have a dance party in your room or watch your favorite TV show. Afterward, compare this experience to how you would normally feel without the music and reward.

I am excited about (an activity you don't usually love).
I give myself permission to feel unlimited amounts of joy.

The sensation of fullness tells you when to slow down or stop eating. If you have been eating emotionally for some time, you may have a complicated relationship with fullness. What does it feel like to be full? Do you listen to your fullness cues or eat past fullness?

Connecting to Your Fullness Scale

By practicing mindful eating and listening to your body, you can learn to eat the amount that is best for you.

Remember that there is no "right" amount of food that can be calculated. Your body knows best what the perfect amount of food is. You can practice connecting with your body by using the fullness scale. During your meals, pause and check in with your fullness.

How full are you on a scale of 0 to 10, 0 being not full at all and 10 being painfully full?

0   1   2   3   4   5   6   7   8   9   10

I listen to my body to tell me how much food to eat. I am not bound by rules or portion sizes.

FOOD APLENTY

If you tend to eat past a comfortable level, there's a chance that you worry about having enough food. Get quiet for a moment and check in with yourself to see if you're eating past fullness because you worry about having access to food later. If you find that this is the case, eat until you are comfortably full and remind yourself that you can eat again later if you get hungry.

It may take time for your body to feel full. If you are unsure if you've had enough, wait about 20 minutes. If you're eating to distract yourself, consider a mindful activity instead.

I can eat until I'm comfortably full. I can eat again later when I'm hungry. There will always be enough food for me.

In this modern age, we're used to always doing *something,* like scrolling and snacking. Do you remember the predigital days when you had lulls and no smartphone to distract your mind? I remember staring at the bathroom floor tiles and making out patterns. Ask yourself: How did I fill my time before this era of constant activity?

Finger Labyrinth

A labyrinth is an intricate path that has been used for meditation and relaxation for thousands of years. Using this continuous version of a labyrinth, try this as one mindful way to ease stress.

Take a breath before you begin. Slowly trace the labyrinth below with your finger, choosing your own starting and ending points. Move your finger slowly and steadily, being mindful not to rush. Once you find yourself calmed, stop tracing. Now, notice what your mind was doing. Were you thinking about something else?

Once you get the hang of it, try it with your non-dominant hand.

I let my mind rest. / I let my thoughts go. / I let my body feel. / I let my worries go free. / I let myself be. / I let myself be.

THE POWER OF BEING PRESENT

The next time you're in line at the grocery store or in the waiting room at the doctor's office, notice how you pass the time. Do you have the urge to pull out your phone? Practice being present instead of checking your messages or doing something "productive."

1. Start by tuning into the surrounding sounds.

2. Then, turn your senses inward and notice your thoughts, feelings, and your body's responses.

3. If you notice you're holding tension, try to relax.

4. Just let yourself be present in the moment.

I am in no rush to be anywhere else or to get anything done. I am perfectly content to be here and taking a breath.

Resources

Intuitive Eating: A Revolutionary Anti-Diet Approach by Evelyn Tribole, MS, RDN, CEDRD-S and Elyse Resch, MS, RDN, CEDRD-S, FAND: Intuitive Eating is a mindful approach to eating that includes how to manage emotions and overcome emotional eating. This book provides ten principles to improve one's relationship with food and their body.

How to Eat by Thich Nhat Hanh: This is a small book full of Buddhist monk Thich Nhat Hanh's simple yet insightful wisdom on eating mindfully.

The Miracle of Mindfulness by Thich Nhat Hanh: Thich Nhat Hanh beautifully illustrates the benefits of mindfulness and how to practice being present in our everyday lives.

Food Liberation, Food-Liberation.com: Food Liberation is a 90-day program created by Mayuko Okai, MS, RD for mindful individuals who are looking for in-depth guidance to heal their relationship with food, connect with their body, and do the things they love most.

Health at Every Size (HAES), HAESCommunity.com: HAES is a movement that encourages inclusive care and body diversity. The website offers a bank of resources, from organizations to podcasts.

The Center for Mindful Eating (TCME), TheCenterForMindfulEating.org: TCME is a nonprofit organization that offers resources to support mindful eating for both professionals and individuals.

References

Agrawal, Radha. *Belong: Find Your People, Create Community, and Live a More Connected Life.* New York: Workman Publishing Company, 2018.

Beauchemin, Molly. "Understanding Ho'oponopono: A Beautiful Hawaiian Prayer for Forgiveness." *Grace & Lightness Magazine.* June 26, 2020. graceandlightness.com/hooponopono-hawaiian -prayer-for-forgiveness.

Floss, Simon. "2 Screens Aren't Better than 1: Danger of Media Multitasking." Sanford Health. June 17, 2020. https://news.sanfordhealth.org/behavioral-health/2-screens -arent-better-than-1-danger-of-media-multitasking/.

Hanh, Thich Nhat. *How to Eat (Mindfulness Essentials).* New York: Parallax Press, 2014.

Hanh, Thich Nhat. *The Miracle of Mindfulness: An Introduction to the Practice of Meditation.* 1st ed. Boston: Beacon Press, 1999.

Pikörn, Isabelle. "The 5-4-3-2-1 Grounding Technique: Manage Anxiety by Anchoring in the Present." Insight Timer Blog. Accessed April 7, 2021. insighttimer.com/blog/54321-grounding-technique.

Rogers, R. D., and S. Monsell. "Costs of a Predictable Switch between Simple Cognitive Tasks." *Journal of Experimental Psychology: General* 124, no. 2 (1995): 207–31. https://doi.org/10.1037 /0096-3445.124.2.207.

Tribole, Evelyn, and Elyse Resch. *Intuitive Eating: A Revolutionary Anti-Diet Approach.* 4th ed. New York: St. Martin's Essentials, 2020.

Tribole, Evelyn, and Elyse Resch. *The Intuitive Eating Workbook: Ten Principles for Nourishing a Healthy Relationship with Food (A New Harbinger Self-Help Workbook).* 1st ed. Oakland, CA: New Harbinger Publications, 2017.

Tucker, Lindsay. "How to Practice Sama Vritti Pranayama (Box Breathing)." *Yoga Journal*, June 27, 2019. www.yogajournal.com /practice/sama-vritti-pranayama.

About the Author

 **Mayuko Okai, MS, RD,** is a registered dietitian, yoga teacher, and founder of Food Liberation, a coaching program that helps mindful individuals heal their relationship with food and their bodies. While working eight years across hospitals in Los Angeles, Mayuko pursued yoga teacher training, which opened the doors to a world of healing she had yet to explore. This inspired her to leave her career and shift her nutrition practice, incorporating mindfulness techniques with a focus on emotional care.

Today, Mayuko takes delight in guiding clients from across the globe in finding food freedom so they can live their full lives. In 2021, she founded a scholarship to provide accessible services to teenagers. Mayuko can be found practicing Ashtanga yoga, eating to her heart's desire, and spending time in the countryside of Japan, where she now resides.

CPSIA information can be obtained
at www.ICGtesting.com
Printed in the USA
JSHW040907180821
17952JS00003B/4

9 781648 764875